PROVING YOUR LIBRARY'S VALUE

Persuasive, Organized, and Memorable Messaging

A **UNITED FOR LIBRARIES** ACTION PLANNER

ALAN FISHEL
JILLIAN WENTWORTH

CHICAGO / 2020

ALA Neal-Schuman purchases fund advocacy, awareness,
and accreditation programs for library professionals worldwide.

The E's of Libraries®
What's Your E?®

The E's of Libraries Task Force, a task force of United for Libraries, did much of the work that made this book possible. Thank you to 2018–2019 United for Libraries President Skip Dye, a champion of The E's of Libraries.

The E's of Libraries Task Force:
- Alan Fishel, Partner, Arent Fox (Chair)
- Todd Carpenter, Executive Director, National Information Standards Organization; Board Member, Foundation for Baltimore County (MD) Public Library
- Sara Charlton, Director, Tillamook County (OR) Library
- Chris Culp, Public Services Division Director, Alachua County (FL) Library District
- Nicolle Davies, Assistant Commissioner, State Library, State of Colorado
- Mark Miller, Board Member, Library of Virginia
- Rebecca Miller, Editorial Director, *Library Journal* and *School Library Journal*
- Steven Potter, Library Director and CEO, Mid-Continent Public Library (MO)
- Charity Tyler, Executive Director, Cedar Rapids (IA) Public Library Foundation
- Jillian Wentworth, Manager of Marketing and Membership, United for Libraries (Staff Liaison)

© 2020 by the American Library Association

Extensive effort has gone into ensuring the reliability of the information in this book; however, the publisher makes no warranty, express or implied, with respect to the material contained herein.

ISBNs
978-0-8389-4741-8 (paper)
978-0-8389-4800-2 (PDF)

Library of Congress Control Number: 2020015697

Book design by Kim Thornton in the Tisa Pro and Rift typefaces.

♾ This paper meets the requirements of ANSI/NISO Z39.48-1992 (Permanence of Paper).

Printed in the United States of America
24 23 22 21 20   5 4 3 2 1

United for Libraries: The Association of Library Trustees, Advocates, Friends and Foundations is a division of the American Library Association with approximately 4,000 personal and group members representing hundreds of thousands of library supporters. United for Libraries supports those who govern, promote, advocate, and fundraise for libraries, and brings together library Trustees, Advocates, Friends and Foundations into a partnership that creates a powerful force for libraries in the twenty-first century.

www.ala.org/united

Contents

Introduction: The Answer to "Why Do We Still Need Libraries?" . . . v

---

CHAPTER 1
Overcoming Hurdles to Library Advocacy
1

CHAPTER 2
The E's of Libraries Framework
Education, Employment, Entrepreneurship, Engagement, and Empowerment
11

CHAPTER 3
The E's of Libraries Checklist
Real-World Examples
17

CHAPTER 4
Your Library in Their Language
How to Tailor The E's of Libraries for Your Library and Community
27

CHAPTER 5
Meeting Your Goals with The E's of Libraries
43

Conclusion: The E's of Your Library and Beyond . . .55

Additional Resources . . . 56

About the Authors . . .57

Introduction

The Answer to "Why Do We Still Need Libraries?"

IF YOU ARE A LIBRARIAN OR A LIBRARY ADMINISTRATOR, CHANCES ARE A SIGnificant part of your job involves advocacy and educating the public about what your library does. If you are a library advocate—or part of a library Board of Trustees, a Friends of the Library group, or on the board or staff of a library Foundation—you probably also have to explain what the library does in the community, and why you support it. How many times have you heard the question: "Why do we still need libraries?"

There are many ways to answer this question, but in this book we walk you through what we have found is the most effective way to do so: persuasive, organized, and memorable messaging that any library advocate can adapt to any audience. This customizable framework uses what we call "The E's of Libraries"—Education, Employment, Entrepreneurship, Engagement, and Empowerment—as a starting point to give you the tools you need to prove your library's value to the community in a persuasive, organized, and memorable way.

This book features several exercises that you can complete individually or in a group. These exercises, along with examples of The E's of Libraries in action, will help you determine the E's that are relevant to your library, how to use the E's in your library and community, and how to use the E's for outreach, publicity, partnerships, fundraising, and more.

You'll learn how to overcome the obstacles that library advocates typically face, and how to effectively and persuasively talk about why your library is essential. You'll discover how to talk about your library using the language of your audience, and how to meet your goals using the customizable framework of The E's of Libraries.

A Note about "The E's of Libraries" vs. "The Es of Libraries"

In this book, as well as in prior presentations and materials about The E's of Libraries, we have chosen to include an apostrophe following the "E" in order to make it clear that what is being referred to is the letter "E" and not "Es" or "es" (the phonetic spelling of the letter "S"). To some the apostrophe may appear to indicate a possessive (which would be a grammatical error). Style guides such as the *Chicago Manual of Style* and the *Associated Press Style Guide* have different rules about usage in this case. Most individuals or groups that use The E's of Libraries are going with the apostrophe, but if you like the concept but not the apostrophe, we encourage you to adopt it as The Es of Libraries. As is the case with The E's of Libraries in general, the framework is entirely adaptable to your own needs and your situation.

CHAPTER 1

Overcoming Hurdles to Library Advocacy

YOU KNOW THAT YOUR LIBRARY IS VITAL TO YOUR COMMUNITY. THE library may offer early literacy programs to preschoolers, help job-seekers find training and resources, and provide a valuable hub for the community.

But how do you communicate your library's importance to stakeholders in a way they will find persuasive when you are saying it, *and* in such a way that they will still remember it later? How often do you face opposition to the library, or a general lack of knowledge about what the library does, from those who you think should know?

Do you ever hear any of the following statements?

> "We don't need the library because everything is available online."
> "Libraries are obsolete."
> "I don't need the library, so why should my money support it?"
> "Libraries may be nice to have, but they are hardly essential, and we need to focus our support on what is essential."

Whether you are a librarian, library staff member, a library Trustee, part of a Friends of the Library group, or part of a library Foundation, you have probably heard, and been frustrated by, one or more of these comments. No doubt you have a reply, but before responding, it's crucial to know this: you are hearing these comments because of a gap in understanding that presents you with two major hurdles to overcome.

In order to most effectively change the dynamic around these perceptions and conversations, it's critical to know that libraries face a Reality-Perception Gap.

What Is the Reality-Perception Gap?

1. Perception: Far too many people view libraries as either "nice to have" or "obsolete."
2. Reality: Libraries are not "obsolete," nor are they merely "nice to have," given that they provide essential services in the areas of Education, Employment, Entrepreneurship, Engagement, and Empowerment.

Why Does the Reality-Perception Gap Exist?

The gap is the result of two major hurdles that libraries face in connection with public perception: (1) the "past perception" hurdle, and (2) the "lack of a single dominant activity" hurdle.

1. The "past perception" hurdle:
   - Many people view libraries based on their past perceptions—they see libraries as a good place to go to borrow books, or quietly study, but believe that they are now largely outdated.
   - Other people have the view that libraries are primarily about providing information, but they think that any information they need can now be found online. These people view libraries as being far less important than they were before the widespread use of the internet.

2. The "lack of a single dominant activity" hurdle:
   - Libraries do many great things; they do not, however, have one dominant activity.
   - Most entities that are viewed as essential have *one* dominant activity (e.g., schools educate, and hospitals heal).

It may be helpful for you to know that these are widespread, engrained views and perceptions, and that you are not alone in facing them. People may not always tell you that these are the reasons why they believe libraries are not essential, but often these views are the problem, whether or not they are explicitly expressed. It might be frustrating that so many people don't view libraries as essential. The good news is that by applying the right strategies, you can overcome these hurdles, position yourself in a crucial way to advocate for your library, and have stakeholders on your side in viewing the library as a key entity in the community.

What Is the Reality-Perception Gap regarding the Library in Your Community?

Ask yourself the following questions to determine what hurdles you need to overcome to ensure that your library is viewed as essential:

01 What are some common misperceptions you hear or read about your library?

_____

_____

_____

02 What are some of the positive things you hear or read about your library from your community members and/or stakeholders?

_____

_____

_____

03 What are your library's 3–5 dominant activities?

_____

_____

_____

_____

To overcome the Reality-Perception Gap, the past perception hurdle, and the lack of a single dominant activity hurdle, you need more than just a reply; you need a memorable message that will change the public's perceptions. Perhaps as a "message" you have heard:

"We love libraries."
"Libraries do so much."
"Libraries are essential."

These statements may all be true, but they are not specific or targeted. What is most effective is a strong messaging framework that addresses both the past perception hurdle and the lack of a single dominant activity hurdle. A messaging framework is structured and shows the value of your organization. The E's of Libraries is a messaging framework—the main framework we refer to in this book is structured by "Education, Employment, Entrepreneurship, Engagement, and Empowerment," but as you will see these can be customized. There are several advantages to using a messaging framework:

- A messaging framework makes it far easier for people to remember what libraries do—and that what they do is essential. Once people realize the services libraries perform, and they learn what libraries do in a peruasive, organized, and memorable way, they will know the truth that libraries are essential.
- A messaging framework can turn what would otherwise be a negative when it comes to messaging—the lack of one dominant activity—into a positive.
- A messaging framework will facilitate the way librarians describe what they do through a more consistent structure, and will likely help to increase the number of library advocates.

What Specific Attributes Should Your Library's Messaging Framework Have?

 It must be Memorable: The message itself must be novel, catchy, and creative, and must make it easier for people to remember what libraries and librarians do. Just like an advertisement, your message must stick in your audience's mind.

 It must be Perception-Changing: The messaging must be perception-changing so that libraries can overcome the "past perception" hurdle and the "lack of a single dominant activity" hurdle. The framework must make people think about libraries in a way they haven't done previously.

It must be Actionable: People are more likely to remember and respond to interactive messaging. Again, you should consider advertising that compels or invites its audience to take an action.

This is where The E's of Libraries comes in.

The E's of Libraries is a messaging framework to explain the value of libraries. Much of what libraries do falls into these five categories:

- Education
- Employment
- Entrepreneurship
- Engagement
- Empowerment

The E's of Libraries is:

- **Memorable** because the five categories above are "E" words, so anyone familiar with them can quickly call them to mind.
- **Perception-Changing** because the framework emphasizes what libraries do in all five of the "E's" categories, and can thereby change common misconceptions people have about libraries. The E's emphasize that libraries do many essential things.
- **Actionable** because it's a way to organize your messaging about libraries in an engaging, interactive way. It's a way to talk to those outside the "library world" in their language. Most everyone will say that one or more of these E's is critically important.

Using The E's of Libraries as a framework for your messaging is advantageous both externally and internally.

External Advantages

UNDERSTANDABLE

This messaging consists of terms that are very familiar and understandable to both people in the library community and those outside of the library community.

To effectively advocate for your library, you must tell the story of your library "in their language." That is, if you are talking to someone in the business community, you should explain how the library fosters economic growth (providing resources for entrepreneurs, offering free computer classes, hosting job fairs, etc.). You should meet them where they are and customize your messaging to what's important to them.

SUPPORTABLE

This messaging focuses on the types of activities that potential funders and prospective business partners want to support.

It's all about justifying the money the local government provides to your library, as well the money provided by your donors. What is the payoff for providing this support? The fact that your library is equipping community members with workforce readiness, creating incubation centers for entrepreneurs, offering English for Speakers of Other Languages (ESOL) classes, presenting cultural programming, or hosting a local candidate forum is very attractive to both community leaders and donors.

ESSENTIAL

The categories of activities that comprise The E's of Libraries are generally viewed as essential, and not nice-to-have or obsolete.

Education, Employment, Entrepreneurship, Engagement, and Empowerment are probably all important in your community, and your library is probably a key resource in more than one, or maybe even in all of these areas.

MEMORABLE

This messaging helps people outside of the library community learn what libraries do in a way that they are far more likely to remember.

The key thing to know about library advocacy is to remember that you're not "preaching to the choir"—you must abandon the assumption that everyone knows that library storytimes are crucial for kindergarten readiness, or that it's common knowledge that librarians help job-seekers every day. Most people don't know these facts, or don't know why they're important. The E's of Libraries will help you show people this, and help them remember it.

Internal Advantages

USING A COMMON LANGUAGE

This messaging allows both people in the library community and those supporting the library community to use a common language to discuss the specific areas and activities in which libraries engage.

There are more than 16,000 public libraries (and library systems) in the United States. Imagine the strength they would have if they all used the same messaging. This may not be possible, but getting all the libraries in your district, county, or even state to use the same messaging would be a very powerful thing. (The Maryland Library Association used "The E's of Libraries" framework for their Maryland Library Legislative Day in 2019.)

Even within your library, the library staff, the Board of Trustees, the Friends group, and the library Foundation may all be using different messaging around the library. The E's of Libraries allows each group to be on the same page and to use consistent messaging for all of their outreach and materials.

EASY

The framework embedded in this messaging makes it much easier for the library community, and those supporting the library community, to successfully engage in advocacy on behalf of libraries. The five E's are easy to remember, and even easier to communicate.

Remember:
Don't tell them what you want to say.
Tell them what they need to know.

 # What's Essential to Your Library and Your Community?

Get started by determining what E's-related messaging you should be using. Examine what messaging you've used thus far, and then consider what the key E's are in your community, and how your library supports them. This will give you a basis to delve further into the E's in the next chapter.

What is the current messaging that your library is using?
What have you used in the past?

Which of The E's of Libraries would you consider important in your community?
Rank them in order of most important to least important.

1.
2.
3.
4.
5.

EDUCATION | EMPLOYMENT | ENTREPRENEURSHIP | ENGAGEMENT | EMPOWERMENT

Explain why you have ranked The E's of Libraries in the way you did.

_____
_____
_____
_____
_____

Which of The E's of Libraries does your library support?

What are some E's your library doesn't currently support? Are they important to your community, and if so, in what ways could you support them?

"We tell new board members: 'Employers want graduates who can find and use information effectively, and here's how the library supports information literacy.' . . . This quickly gets them beyond 'past perceptions' and focused on our core mission." —*Heather Craven, County College of Morris, Randolph, NJ*

CHAPTER 2

The E's of Libraries Framework

Education, Employment, Entrepreneurship, Engagement, and Empowerment

AS YOU EXPLORE THE WAYS IN WHICH YOUR LIBRARY IS VITAL TO THE community through the lens of The E's of Libraries, it's helpful to consider what many libraries offer in each category. Here is a basic framework that includes what each "E" may cover, along with general supporting statistics about what public libraries do in each area.

Education

Libraries are vital centers for lifelong learning. Storytimes and other early literacy programs provide critical training for both parents and children when it comes to school readiness. For K–12 students, libraries provide homework help, STEM programming, makerspaces, and summer reading programs to fight the "summer slide." For adults, the library offers ESOL or basic literacy classes, technology training, and more.

- Early learning
- K–12
- Adult

SUPPORTING STATISTICS

K–12 students receive great support from public libraries with regard to homework and information technology access. About 70 percent of parents report that their children use the public library, and 77 percent of student library users aged 12–17 use the library for homework.[1] About 98 percent of public libraries provide formal or informal technology training to patrons.

Employment

From assisting with resumes and job applications to hosting job fairs and networking events, libraries support both those who are looking for employment and those seeking to build their skills.

- Self-evaluation
- Skill-building
- Finding and landing a job

SUPPORTING STATISTICS

Every day 300,000 Americans get job-seeking help at their public library. About 76 percent of public libraries help people complete job applications online, and 92 percent of libraries provide access to online job databases and resources.

Entrepreneurship

Many public libraries help support entrepreneurs in their community. They provide training programs for those starting a new business, and they support those seeking to fund or grow a business by helping them identify funding and investment opportunities.

- Area of interest exploration
- Making connections
- Resources for funding and growing your business

SUPPORTING STATISTICS

According to the University of Maryland's Digital Inclusion Survey (https://digitalinclusion.umd.edu), most public libraries (about 99 percent) report providing economic/workforce services. Of those, about 48 percent report providing entrepreneurship and small business development services. Business owners and employees use the resources at public libraries to support their small businesses 2.8 million times every month.

Engagement

Civic literacy and engagement have increasingly become a priority for libraries, as they host candidate forums and encourage voting and community participation. In addition, libraries present programs that offer both social opportunities and personal enrichment, such as book clubs, author programs, concerts, and so on. Libraries also frequently offer a venue for festivals and community celebrations.

- Learning
- Social
- Community

SUPPORTING STATISTICS

The Public Libraries Survey, conducted by the Institute of Museum and Library Services in 2016, reported that public libraries across the United States presented 5.2 million programs that year, an increase of 72 percent since 2010.[2]

"The public library is a hub of civic engagement, fostering new relationships and strengthening the human capital of the community," states the Aspen Institute's 2014 report, "Rising to the Challenge: Re-Envisioning Public Libraries" (http://csreports.aspeninstitute.org/documents/AspenLibrariesReport.pdf).[3] "Librarians are actively engaged in the community. They connect individuals to a vast array of local and national resources and serve as neutral conveners to foster civic health. They facilitate learning and creation for children and adults alike."[4]

Empowerment

The library offers opportunities for personal advancement to all, and perhaps most crucially to underserved populations. Outreach programs offer access to books for those who can't visit the library, and meal programs for youth and seniors. Increasingly, libraries are hiring social workers and/or linking with social service organizations in the community.

- Financial and health literacy
- Civic, legal, and technical literacy
- Support to underserved populations

SUPPORTING STATISTICS

Libraries facilitate e-health activities. Each year millions of people use library computers to research health and wellness issues, including learning about medical conditions, medical procedures, and diet and nutrition; finding health care providers; and assessing health insurance options.[5]

Libraries provide important e-government services. About 97 percent of public libraries help people apply for government services online.

Other "E's of Libraries"

The E's of Libraries are fully customizable. If you don't see one of the above E's as playing a key role in your community, you need not use it. If there is another "E" that you think is more important, use that one in your framework. For example, perhaps "Equity" is a major value in your urban library, where many patrons are affected by the digital divide. Maybe you want to combine "Employment" and "Entrepreneurship" and use "Economy" instead.

In addition, while Education, Employment, Entrepreneurship, Engagement, and Empowerment are generally applicable to public libraries, they may not be the perfect fit for your school, college, or other library. Perhaps your school library might use Education, Empowerment, Engagement, Equity, and E-Learning. Maybe your university library's E's also include Expertise, E-Learning, and Exploration. You are the expert on your library's strengths and what will resonate with your community.

SOME OTHER POSSIBLE E'S

- Enrichment
- Exploration
- E-Learning

You can also use the E's to discuss other benefits relating to libraries, including:

- Equity (what libraries help create)
- Expertise (what librarians and staff provide)
- Ease (accessibility of the library)
- Everyone (who libraries serve)
- Economy (what libraries support)
- Everywhere (where libraries are)

What Are Your Library's E's?

Use these questions to determine your own library's customized "E's of Libraries" framework:

> As you read over the three basic areas listed under each "E" above, what resonates with you? In what area(s) does your library excel, and in what way?

> What are some unique qualities of your library and/or community to consider as you adapt "The E's of Libraries" framework to your situation?

What are some additional E's (beyond the basic five) that may be applicable for your library to incorporate into its E's messaging? How are they applicable? What does your library do to support these additional E's?

NOTES

1. All of the statistics in this chapter except the one in note 2 are from the sources listed here: www.ilovelibraries.org/es-libraries-source-materials.

2. NILPPA: National Impact of Library Public Programs Assessment, https://nilppa.org/wp-content/uploads/2019/06/NILPPA_Phase-1-white-paper.pdf.

3. Aspen Institute, "Rising to the Challenge: Re-Envisioning Public Libraries," October 2014, http://csreports.aspeninstitute.org/documents/AspenLibrariesReport.pdf.

4. American Library Association, www.ala.org/news/sites/ala.org.news/files/content/state-of-americas-libraries-2016-final.pdf.

5. Institute of Museum and Library Services, www.imls.gov/news/us-impact-study-second-report-opportunity-all-how-library-policies-and-practices-impact-public.

CHAPTER 3

The E's of Libraries Checklist

Real-World Examples

A S YOU THINK ABOUT THE E'S OF LIBRARIES AND YOUR LIBRARY, TAKE A look at the corresponding examples of services provided by libraries under each "E," as given below. This will give you rich examples to draw from when developing your customized E's framework. Check the ones that apply to your library, and add additional services as needed.

Education

EARLY CHILDHOOD LEARNING
- ☐ Reading to children
- ☐ Helping children learn how to socialize with others
- ☐ Providing learning strategies for parents to use at home
- ☐ Other _____

K–12 EDUCATION
- ☐ Homework support
- ☐ Supplementing the school curriculum with technology, active learning, and experiences
- ☐ Fighting the "summer slide"
- ☐ Other _____

ADULT EDUCATION
- ☐ Adult reading and literacy classes
- ☐ High school diploma equivalency courses or GED
- ☐ Supporting college or community college education
- ☐ Other _____

Employment

SELF-EVALUATION
- ☐ Helping patrons understand what skills they have
- ☐ Helping patrons understand what skills they need
- ☐ Helping patrons understand how to go about obtaining those skills
- ☐ Other _____

SKILL BUILDING
- ☐ Free classes and educational programs
- ☐ Access to online training and expert guidance
- ☐ Collections and materials
- ☐ Other _____

FINDING AND LANDING THE JOB
- ☐ Resume preparation support
- ☐ Job search resources and job fairs
- ☐ Application completion support, interview training programs
- ☐ Other _____

Entrepreneurship

AREA OF INTEREST EXPLORATION
- ☐ Access to online content and databases and expert guidance
- ☐ Collections and materials
- ☐ Business training programs
- ☐ Other _____

FACILITATING CONNECTIONS
- ☐ Identifying social networks and peer groups
- ☐ Social media training
- ☐ Connecting with applicable government officials and regulators
- ☐ Other _____

IDENTIFYING RESOURCES FOR FUNDING AND GROWING YOUR BUSINESS
- ☐ Assistance in drafting business or marketing plans
- ☐ Identifying potential venture capitalists and private investors
- ☐ Identifying potential government or other public funding sources and grant opportunities
- ☐ Other _____

Engagement

LEARNING
- ☐ Cooking, sewing, dance, exercise, art, writing, and life skills classes
- ☐ Makerspaces and STEM centers
- ☐ Educational competitions, human libraries
- ☐ Other _____

SOCIAL
- ☐ Book clubs, author visits, and book club kits
- ☐ Meeting room or venue for celebrations, performances, and networking
- ☐ Social services hub (housing, mental health, welfare)
- ☐ Other _____

COMMUNITY
- ☐ Town halls, candidate forums, debates, voting and ballot drop-off locations
- ☐ Festivals and cultural events
- ☐ Outreach to community to help define needs and gaps
- ☐ Other _____

Empowerment

FINANCIAL, TECHNOLOGY, AND HEALTH CARE LITERACY
- ☐ Basic budgeting classes, free tax preparation
- ☐ Computer coding classes
- ☐ Free child health screenings and telehealth counseling
- ☐ Other _____

CIVIC AND LEGAL LITERACY
- ☐ E-government access and community information
- ☐ Voter resources
- ☐ Legal aid workshops
- ☐ Other _____

SUPPORT FOR UNDERSERVED POPULATIONS
- ☐ English language learning classes
- ☐ Services for veterans
- ☐ Books delivery for the homebound, meal programs for children or seniors
- ☐ Other _____

 ## Picking Your Favorite Stories

Considering how your library makes a real difference in your patrons' lives can help you define your library's E's and the value you bring to people and your community. Spend some time thinking of these stories and then match them with relevant E's.

What are three (or more) of your favorite stories about your library making a difference for those in the community? For each story, what "E" or E's does it involve?

01 E's: _____

_____

THE E'S OF LIBRARIES CHECKLIST / 21

02 E's: _____

03 E's: _____

As you look back on your notes and answers for the section above, try to list three specific examples of services or activities your library provides for each "E":

EDUCATION

EMPLOYMENT

ENTREPRENEURSHIP

THE E'S OF LIBRARIES CHECKLIST / 23

ENGAGEMENT

EMPOWERMENT

OTHER "E'S"

You probably have many powerful stories about how your library supports Education, Employment, Entrepreneurship, Engagement, and Empowerment. Consider the stories below from library directors and librarians about the impact their library makes in the community, and how they relate these stories to The E's of Libraries.

EDUCATION

"Through grant funding this summer, we were able to provide struggling readers with a free day program for six weeks. They received tutoring at school, then walked to the library to participate in our weekly science activities and check out books, with lunch provided by the food pantry. We had paid teachers and volunteers and it was a collaboration of two libraries, the school district, and a food pantry."

—**Lisa Semenza, Hazard Library Association, Poplar Ridge, NY**

EMPLOYMENT

"With a manufacturer closing in town, we partnered with the Wisconsin Department of Workforce Development and employment offices to have classes/sessions at the library to help them get benefits and find new jobs."

—**Dominic, Antigo Public Library, WI**

ENGAGEMENT

"I have a patron who regularly attends my adult craft programs. She informed me about seven months after I started them that she appreciated the opportunities we provide—she had miscarried and was in a very dark place. When she started coming to my programs, it gave her something to look forward to and enjoy."

—**Sarah Scott, Whitehall Public Library, PA**

EMPOWERMENT

"The state of Illinois has a civil, legal self-help system, and my library is the legal self-help center for our county. We also offer fax, copy, scan-to-e-mail, and free notary services. One day, a patron came in to find out if she could make copies at the library. While talking to us, she said that she was going in for a medical procedure that only had a 60 percent survival rate. She was trying to track down an attorney to write up a living will and a notary for some other documents. She was very stressed and understandably so. When we told her she could use our legal self-help center for the living will and we could notarize everything for her, she cried with relief. She was empowered after feeling so helpless."

—Bobbi Perryman, Vespasian Warner Public Library District, Clinton, IL

EMPOWERMENT

"A patron came in having recently escaped an abusive relationship and looking for a place to stay that was safe. Through our community partnerships and previous organization of resources, we were able to give her multiple options and put her in contact with several local places that could help."

—Ensley F. Guffey, Cleveland County Library System, NC

EMPOWERMENT AND EDUCATION

"A mom, who was a recent immigrant going through a divorce and without many friends, was able to use our library's services and make connections with other people to earn her high school diploma. We changed her life and made a difference."

—Sharon Tani, Yolo County Library, CA

CHAPTER 4

Your Library in Their Language

How to Tailor The E's of Libraries for Your Library and Community

AFTER ANSWERING THE QUESTIONS IN THE PREVIOUS CHAPTER, YOU are equipped with some examples, from your point of view, of the E's, and the categories and subcategories within them, that are specific to your library. However, it's key to obtain input from those who work in the library, who advocate for it, and (above all) those who use it. You know what *you* think, but what do *they* think the most important services are that your library offers? How do *they* see the library making a difference in the community?

The following are some ways to get information about what patrons find most useful about your library. We recommend that you incorporate The E's of Libraries into these efforts in order to provide a framework, but if you prefer not to, you may simply use the feedback to inform the campaign you're building around The E's of Libraries.

- If you haven't done so recently, you may wish to conduct surveys or focus groups that incorporate questions about what users most value about the library. (This is also an opportunity for a much broader effort to gauge the community's needs and ensure your library is meeting them.) Ask them for stories about how the library has helped them, their family, or others. Offer a small reward (a gift card, a coupon for the Friends books sale, etc.) to those who participate, if possible, or enter participants into a drawing to win a prize. If there are certain clubs or groups that regularly use your library (e.g.,

a book club group, or a homeschooler meetup), reach out directly to them for their input.
- Reach out to the Friends of the Library, the Board of Trustees, the library Foundation, or all three. Host individual or joint gatherings between these groups. As influential community members not employed by the library, they have a valuable perspective. They know how the library is viewed in the community, and they have links to local influencers and stakeholders. Ask them what they most value about the library, and for stories about how the library has helped them personally or how they see it helping others.
- Host a brainstorming session with the staff if time allows, or schedule a few meetings with some key staff members. Ask the staff for their recent or past success stories. If possible, include staff at all levels and departments, whether or not they work directly with the public or not—those who work at the circulation desk, information technology, security, assistants, and so on. How are they seeing the library make a difference in the community? How do the specific areas they work in make an impact on library users? Offer staff members a chance to tell their stories face-to-face (record them if possible) as well as to submit written stories, in order to accommodate various communication styles.
- Take a look at the statistics you regularly share in making the case for your library. What strengths do they show the library has? If you need a way to collect, analyze, and share this information, the Public Library Association's Project Outcome (www.projectoutcome.org) is a free toolkit designed to help public libraries understand and share the impact of essential library services and programs by providing simple surveys and an easy-to-use process for measuring and analyzing outcomes. The project's outcomes are measured in seven key library service areas—Civic/Community Engagement, Digital Learning, Economic Development, Education/Lifelong Learning, Early Childhood Literacy, Job Skills, and Summer Reading—which will align well with your "E's of Libraries" framework.

The Right "E" for the Occasion

When you go into a meeting, or when you're planning a presentation or talk, remember: you don't need to bring up all of The E's of Libraries to make your case. Use whichever "E" or E's are applicable to the situation, and whichever categories or subcategories within those E's that you need to use.

Your Library Making a Difference

You can incorporate The E's of Libraries in both your storytelling about the library and in the statistics you have that show why the library is important. This exercise will help you identify compelling narratives and impressive statistics that you can use in messaging related to The E's of Libraries.

What are some firsthand stories from library users about how the library has helped them? How does each story incorporate one or more "E's of Libraries"?

How do each of the following groups (if they exist in your library) see the library making a difference in the community?

What are some key statistics about your library that show how it is making a difference in the community in the areas of Education, Employment, Entrepreneurship, Engagement, and Empowerment (or another "E" relevant to your library)?

EDUCATION

EMPLOYMENT

ENTREPRENEURSHIP

ENGAGEMENT

EMPOWERMENT

OTHER "E"

The Key "E's" in Your Community

In addition to analyzing how The E's of Libraries are in action in your library, it will be key to determine what E's are critical in your community. Is your town in need of small business growth, and if so would it be helpful to offer resources for entrepreneurs? Is there a demand for GED classes because of a high school-dropout rate? Is there a large population of seniors, with many in need of engagement opportunities (social opportunities, beginner computer classes, cultural events)? Do many people in your community need ESOL classes or support?

As you begin to build your campaign around The E's of Libraries, you will make a major impact if you can show how the library helps solve the community's problems. Instead of a general message like "The library does so much for this community," you will be able to say something like this: "52 percent of those who responded to a survey about the library's job search services said they could not have found employment without the library, resulting in 158 residents who went from being unemployed to securing a job because of the library."

In addition, thinking about what's important to the community's stakeholders will allow you to craft targeted messages to whoever you're trying to appeal to. If you're making a case for increased library funding to a town manager, think about initiatives and areas that are of critical importance to that person (for example, anything that will improve job readiness and the town's economic health). If you're trying to secure a donation from a large corporation in your community, explain how the library supports that company's employees and their families through lifelong learning opportunities, after-school programs, summer reading, and so on.

The E's in Your Community

What are some key issues or problems facing your community? How do they align with or relate to The E's of Libraries?

___

How does your library assist with some of the problems listed above? What specific library programs or initiatives address these problems?

___

With increased funding or resources, what else could the library do to address the common problems facing community members?

___

Complete the chart below, listing the relevant stakeholders in the community (these may be individuals, groups, businesses, etc.). Identify key issues of importance to them. Add which of The E's of Libraries is relevant to them. Pick a library story and/or a library statistic that would be meaningful to use when meeting with this stakeholder, reaching out to them for increased funding, soliciting a donation, seeking a partnership, and so on.

COMMUNITY STAKEHOLDER/VIP

Their key issue(s)

Library story relating to the E or E's

Corresponding E or E's

Library statistic relating to the E or E's

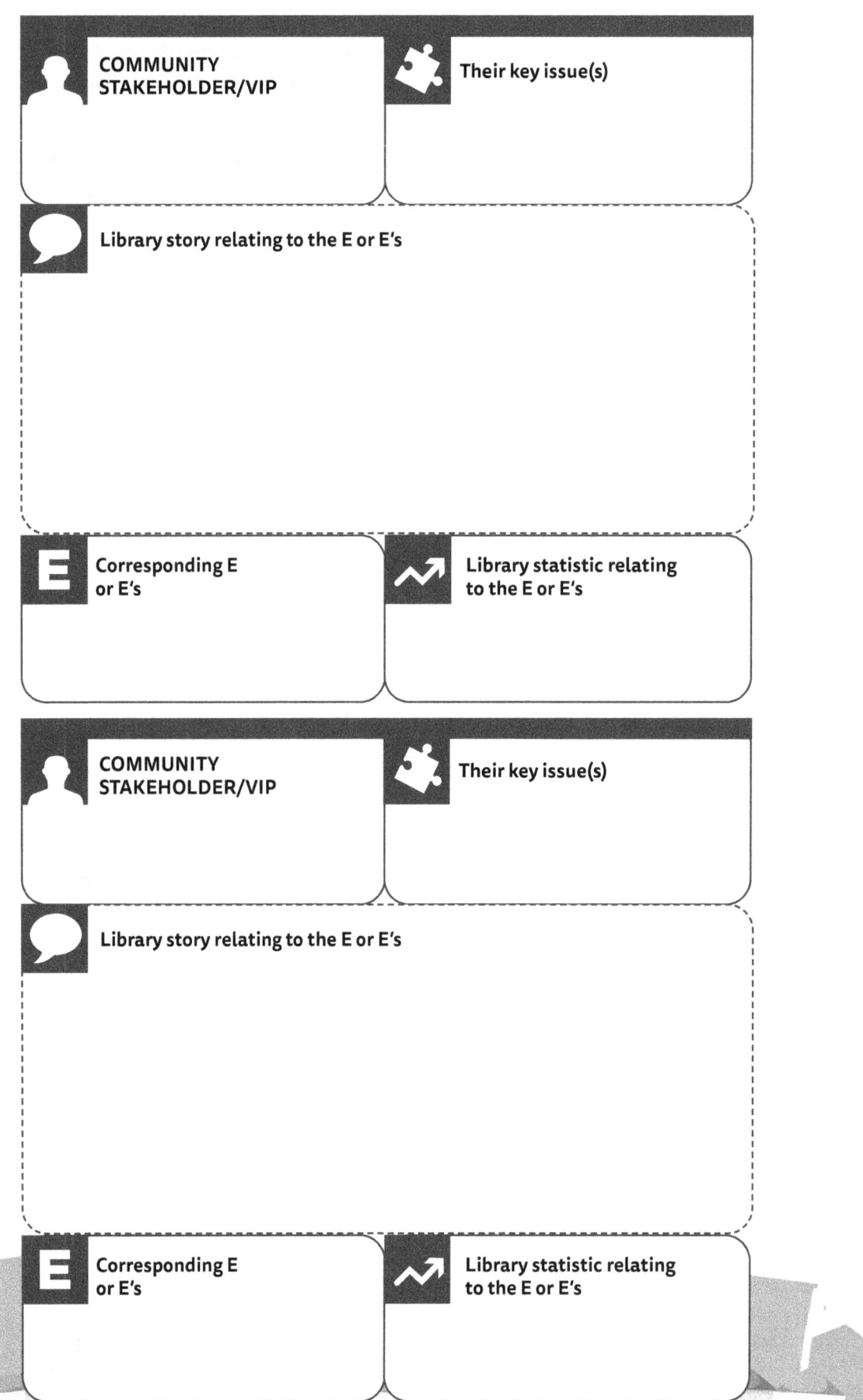

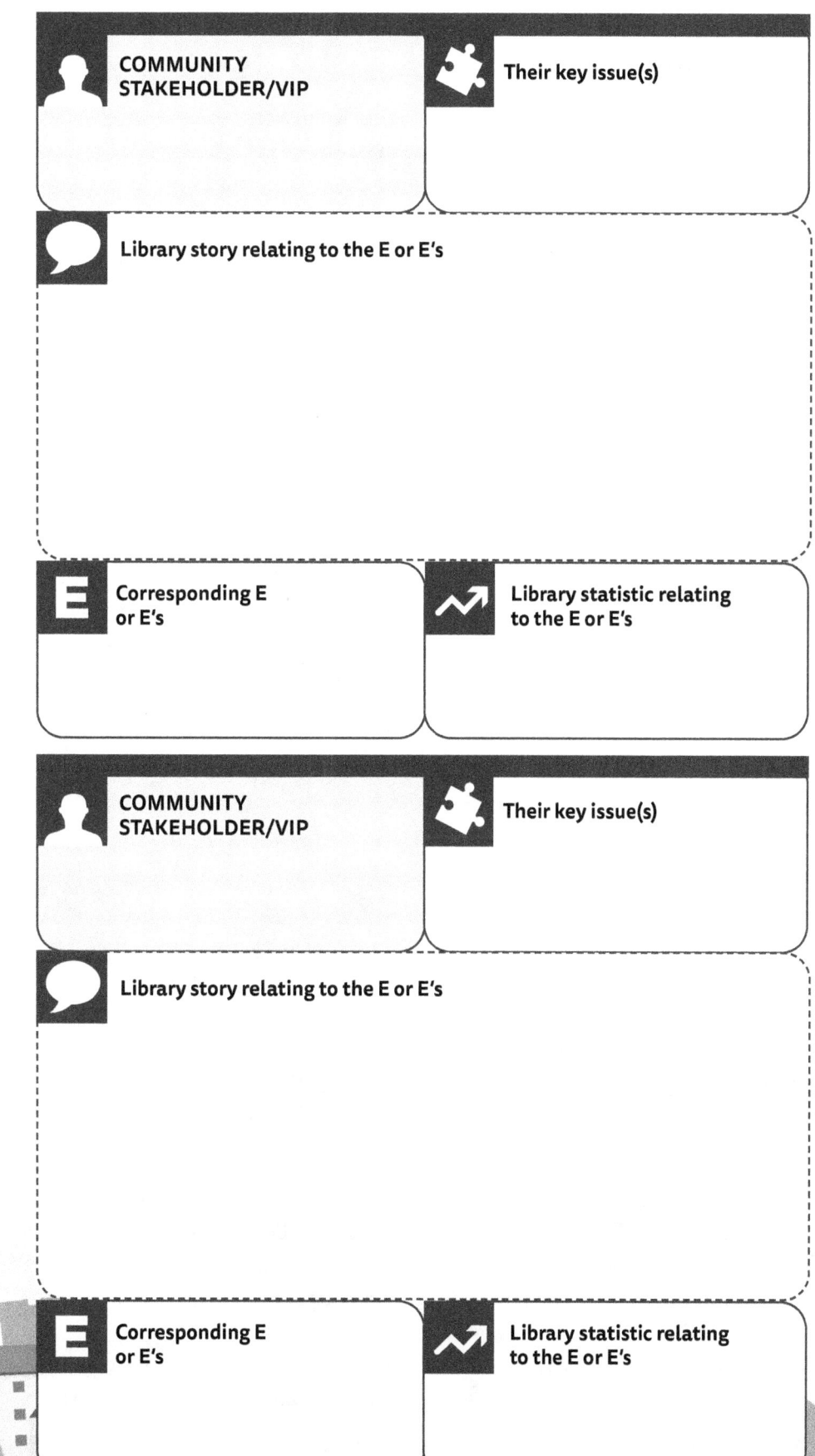

What's Your "E"?

In addition to "The E's of Libraries" messaging framework, you can incorporate "What's Your E?" This is a messaging option that can be used in actionable (interactive) ways. "What's Your E?" is a way to begin a discussion about what libraries do, and immediately find out what is important to the person you are making the case to. It can also be used in promotional and marketing activities.

AMONG LIBRARY STAFF

Which one of The E's of Libraries resonates most with each member of your library staff? Ask them via a quick e-mail or survey—"What's Your E?" You can use these as testimonials about the expertise and enthusiasm of your staff. Consider making name tags or other promotional materials incorporating the "My E is . . ." messaging for staff members.

WITH KEY STAKEHOLDERS

When meeting with someone about the library, explain the library's strengths in terms of The E's of Libraries, and find out what "E" is important to the person you are talking to. A conversation might go like this:

> *Library rep:* "Thanks for meeting with me today about partnering with the library. We have some key initiatives related to Education, Employment, and Empowerment, since those are critical areas in our community right now. Which one of these 'E's' is most important to you and your organization?"
>
> *Community organization rep:* "Well, one of the things our organization does is work with individuals who are recent immigrants, connecting them with

resources in the community. They often feel lost or overwhelmed, so 'Empowerment' really resonates with me."

Library rep: "So your 'E' is 'Empowerment'—that's great! We have library volunteers who conduct English-language discussion groups with ESOL learners, and we have collections of books in languages other than English. Let's talk more about how we can work together...."

ELEVATOR SPEECHES

The E's of Libraries and "What's Your E?" are great to have in the back of your mind as you respond to questions like "Isn't everything on the internet?" and "Why do we still need a library in our community?" When you are well versed in what your library excels at as far as each "E" goes, it's easy to respond to these questions on the fly:

Community member: "You work for the library? Aren't libraries obsolete now that everything's on the internet?"

Library rep: "Actually, in addition to providing access to the internet, our library has expert staff who lead initiatives in the areas of Employment, Entrepreneurship, and Education. What do you think is the most important need in our community right now?"

Community member: "Well, since the manufacturing plant is closing at the end of the year, there are going to be a lot of people looking for jobs."

Library rep: "Good point. The library offers job search training, in addition to resume workshops and basic technology classes."

DONORS

Your donors are probably looking to support something they personally feel strongly about, so a "What's Your E?" approach with them may help you as you make an appeal. Maybe they started their own business, so the fact that the library has an Entrepreneurial Center will resonate with them, or perhaps they come from an arts background and will be impressed by the concerts and author readings your library hosts.

WITH TRUSTEES

Asking Board of Trustees members "What's Your E?" is a great way to get them to think about how they can advocate for the library. This starts a dialogue about what the library does, and the Trustees may learn about library activities they were previously unaware of, and which resonate with them. You will probably also find out about some skills or connections your Trustees have that you may not have known about.

WITH FRIENDS OF THE LIBRARY MEMBERS

Friends of the Library members are often the library's biggest fans. They may wish to use "What's Your E?" messaging while they are out in the community raising funds or working the library's book sale. If you would like your Friends group to go to the "next level"—say, they only do book sales and you want them to take a more active role out in the community and in advocacy initiatives—"What's Your E?" messaging is a great place to start.

FIGURE 4.1
The Brownwood (TX) Public Library incorporated the "My E is . . ." message into a "Libraries Are Essential" flyer about the library while making its case for a budget increase.

The E's in Action: "What's Your E?"

EDUCATION

"In general, I really like *Education* because I feel like we do so much here: coding programs for kids, tech assistance, community lectures, storytimes, book clubs, Science in the Summer for kids, summer reading, informal spaces for quiet study, Spanish story time, STEM toys for kids—all of these programs assist our patrons."

—Robyn Langston, Ludington Library, Bryn Mawr, PA

EMPLOYMENT

"We helped a gentleman use the library's computers to apply for jobs, and the next time we saw him, he was a carpenter on our library building's expansion."

—Holly Williams, Pittsfield Public Library, Pittsfield, ME

EMPOWERMENT

"My library organized Mid City Micro-Con in February 2018. The event celebrated diversity in comic book characters, creators, and fans. Guests told us and our speakers that they never knew there were so many indie creators providing that kind of (diverse) content. One of our cosplayers said that our event was the most memorable of her career of over a decade because of the number of people she—a plus-sized cosplayer—was able to reach and empower."

—Samantha Belmont, East Baton Rouge Parish Library, LA

EDUCATION

"A grandmother started to bring her grandson to storytime. After a few weeks, she came up to me and told me how grateful she was for our programs. Her grandson had been having speech problems and, after coming to storytime, he was talking more, socializing, and repeating the songs at home. She has come up a few times since then, telling me how much he has improved. She gets teary and so do I."

—Sheila Olson, Altoona Public Library, IA

ENGAGEMENT

"I'm a teen librarian, so I like to think my programs involve all the E's! I love the connections being made between 'my' kids—the seventh graders and the high schoolers, the homeschoolers and the public school kids. They're engaging with each other and being empowered to learn new things, form opinions, and challenge each other and the norm! I love every exhausting minute!"

—Emily Linacre, Altoona Public Library, IA

ENTREPRENEURSHIP

"Our Teen Tycoons program is a teen entrepreneurship program that teaches kids finance, money management, college costs, entrepreneurship, and so on. We have a partnership with SCORE Houston—they mentor and counsel students and small businesses. All this at the library!"

—Milagros Tanega, Evelyn Meador Library, Seabrook, TX

CHAPTER 5

Meeting Your Goals with The E's of Libraries

DEPENDING ON YOUR ROLE WITH THE LIBRARY—WHETHER YOU ARE A director, staff member, part of the Board, Friends, or Foundation, or in some other role—you will use the E's in different ways. The library and its support groups can launch a coordinated initiative in how they will use The E's of Libraries. Perhaps you will use The E's of Libraries as part of a district- or county-wide coordinated effort, in a statewide effort, or even when you're reaching out to your representatives on the national level. The E's of Libraries are adaptable and versatile: to see how you can best use them, take a look at your goals for the library or support group. Below are some ways you might adapt The E's of Libraries to fit your needs.

Library Administrators

MAKING THE CASE TO FUNDERS

Incorporate The E's of Libraries into your budget presentations to create a memorable message about everything that your library does in the community. Create a one-pager about the library featuring the E's, so that you can leave it behind when visiting the mayor, city council members, and others.

ENGAGING COMMUNITY PARTNERS

Show local organizations and businesses how the library supports their needs and missions by showcasing the E's that are relevant to them. You can even create targeted materials for each "E" to promote what the library does in that area.

MARKETING

Use The E's of Libraries in your marketing materials, in social media, and on your

> "As the director of the Tillamook (OR) County Library and a member of The E's of Libraries Task Force, I was probably one of the first people to test the E's for publicity purposes. First, I used the E's when talking to my representatives for National Library Legislative Day. As I discussed how federal funding helped my library, I used each "E," and this worked perfectly for the five minutes I had to talk about public libraries and my library. I also used the E's in my talks to my local commissioners, on TV, to local organizations, and to library boards. People understood as I talked about the E's. It was great PR because I could change it to make it specific to my library if needed, or keep the E's on a broad level to talk about libraries in general."
>
> —Sara Charlton, Director, Tillamook County Library, OR

website. Create a parallel "What's Your E?" campaign. Design a flyer featuring the E's and pass it out at library programs (storytimes, book club meetings, technology classes), so library users will get an idea of the library's full spectrum of services.

The E's in Action: Baltimore County Public Library

"As with many libraries across the country, in addition to our traditional services, we have added a number of social and community services to the mix of what we provide to the community. How do we explain all that we do in a concise and very understandable way? When I first heard about The E's of Libraries, I thought those could be our 'buckets' that we use to explain in a substantive way what our libraries are all about. They are easy to understand for the community, funders, and legislators, and they're also easy to remember for our staff and our board when we're out in groups doing presentations or just networking and talking with people."—**Paula Miller, Director, Baltimore County (MD) Public Library**

In 2018, the Baltimore County (MD) Public Library began featuring The E's of Libraries in several different ways—selecting Education, Economy, Equity, and Engagement as its four E's to highlight. Figure 5.1 (at right) is the introduction to their budget request for that year, and a brief explanation of why and how they selected their E's.

MEETING YOUR GOALS WITH THE E'S OF LIBRARIES / 45

> "We had existing partnerships with the school system, and that has been a traditional support area of service that public libraries have provided."

INNOVATION and PARTNERSHIPS: Collective Impact

The Library leverages partnerships with County and State agencies, nonprofits and local businesses in order to extend the reach of library services and resources. Collaborative programming allows for innovative ideas to reach wider audiences; cross-promotion ensures greater return on investment, and greater access to resources means more opportunity for Baltimore County residents.

EDUCATION

- All **115,000** BCPS students now have automatic **Student Accounts** with BCPL. These accounts can be used to check out materials, utilize research databases; and, best of all, do not accrue fines; eliminating a barrier to access.
- More than **50,000** children participate in the **Summer Reading** program each year, which provides fun and accessible ways to connect to reading and learning throughout the summer, keeping children better prepared for the start of a new school year.
- Librarians from the Parkville Branch maintain a close relationship with the **Hickey School**, providing regular book discussion visits at this youth detention center. In support of this program, BCPL has won funding through an ALA Great Stories grant.
- Partnering with **Towson University** has enabled a variety of collaborative programs, including professors speaking at programs, BC Reads events hosted on the TU Campus and book discussions in support of TU grant projects.

ECONOMY

- The **William & Lanaea C. Featherstone Foundation** provides workforce and technical training for Latino and underserved customers.
- The **Maryland Small Business Development Center, Small Business Administration** and **CASH Campaign** work with the library to provide workshops at several branches that support the development and success of entrepreneurs, solopreneurs and small businesses.
- Librarians assist customers daily with online job applications, learning new job skills and interview tips.
- CASH Campaign of Maryland will provide personal finance classes and free tax preparation for low-income customers in FY19. Funding for the tax preparation service is provided in part by grants from Wells Fargo and PNC.

EQUITY

- Summer lunches and after-school snacks are provided at no cost to the library or to the children. More than **27,000** meals and snacks were served in FY18 alone.
- **Maryland Legal Aid** provides free, drop-in legal assistance with civil matters at various branches.
- A grant from the **Maryland State Library** enabled BCPL to offer the "Build Your Own Computer" series at two branches. Presented by **Baltimore Robotics Club**, participants learned to build their own computer, which they were able to keep at the end of the program.
- **Social justice programs** bring participants together with local authors, artists, activists and leaders. Our branches provide safe spaces for conversation and thoughtful discourse on challenging issues.
- **E-devices**, including Google Chromebooks, are now circulated to make technology accessible to all Baltimore County residents.

ENGAGEMENT

- Librarians visit **WIC Centers** to promote early learning practices and spread awareness of library services.
- Held in April, the annual **BC Reads** program promotes community-wide discussion through reading and the arts.
- **Baltimore County Health and Human Services** provides smoking cessation, diabetes education and Narcan trainings at various branches.
- The Library provides book clubs, technology instruction and mobile library services at **County Senior Centers**.
- Collaboration with **Baltimore County Department of Recreation & Parks** to provide off-site library services through Talking is Teaching panels, Story Trails and Little Free Libraries.

> "We chose *economy* to encapsulate both Employment, which is job fill, and Entrepreneurship, which is job creation. We see those needs daily with individuals coming through our doors."

> "This choice was very much driven by the values of our organization. It has been a strong value for us and an area in which we've been providing more services and looking at more closely."

> "One of the objectives in our strategic plan is to serve as an instrument of democracy for our community. *Engagement* captures civic and community engagement. And our vision statement is 'Empowered and engaged individuals for a more inclusive and connected Baltimore County community.'"

FIGURE 5.1
The introduction to the Baltimore County Public Library's 2018 budget request featured their four E's. The library director, Paula Miller, explained why they decided to use each one.

The Baltimore County Public Library tailored The E's of Libraries in other ways as well:
- In a presentation to the Chamber of Commerce (emphasizing the library's role in the economy and its impact)
- In a legislative breakfast at one of the libraries to discuss the E's and talk about what was going on in the library
- In a presentation to the Baltimore County government planning board
- In grant applications
- To talk about general quality of life and safety issues (everyone, everywhere)
- In the library's annual report
- In elevator speeches
- In a transition document to inform a new county executive about the library's initiatives and areas of focus
- In conjunction with other phrases:
    » "Libraries are a smart investment" (Education)
    » "Libraries mean business" (Economy)
    » "Libraries change lives" (Equity)
    » "Libraries build community" (Engagement)

The E's in Action: Board of Trustees

ADVOCATING IN THE COMMUNITY

Use The E's of Libraries as an entry point to get your Board of Trustees advocating for the library in the community and beyond. The E's can help them develop talking points for library advocacy, and their advocacy efforts as community members will amplify the message.

BOARD DEVELOPMENT

Doing a "What's Your E?" exercise among board members will provide an easy way to discover board members' skills that you may not have already identified, and to determine how board members can help the library with specific advocacy initiatives, funding efforts, or connections in the community.

STRATEGIC PLANNING AND POLICY

When the board is discussing policy changes, strategic planning, determining a mission or vision statement, future initiatives for the library, and other topics, use The E's of Libraries as a reference for the library's current strengths, what opportunities the library might have, and as a reminder for what the library's goals and initiatives are.

The E's in Action: Mission and Vision Statements

Your library's mission or vision/value statement may already include one or more of The E's of Libraries. A few examples of these mission statements (with the E's emphasized) are given below. For a tip sheet for your Board of Trustees on writing mission statements, visit www.ala.org/united/trusteezone/tipsheets (United for Libraries member log-in required).

MISSION

Rochester (NY) Public Library: "We create a community of readers and *empower* individuals with free access to information and the universe of ideas."

MISSION

Madison (WI) Public Library: "The Madison Public Library provides free and equitable access to cultural and *educational* experiences. We celebrate ideas, promote creativity, connect people, and enrich lives."

VISION

Portland (ME) Public Library: "Portland Public Library will be the civic and cultural center of a dynamic region in which citizens are literate, informed, and *engaged*. The Library will provide resources and experiences that inspire imagination, curiosity, awareness, and learning. The Library will embrace change and evolve to meet the needs of the community."

The E's in Action: Library Foundations

CRAFTING A COMPELLING CASE

When creating your Foundation's case for support, use The E's of Libraries as a framework. Identify which E's in particular the Foundation supports—and what other E's the Foundation could support with more funding. You may also use or reference The E's of Libraries in grant applications.

ANNUAL APPEALS

Your Foundation can use The E's of Libraries in its funding appeal letters, e-mails, and other materials. The E's are an ideal framework for providing an easy-to-read, scannable letter or mail piece that will quickly give potential donors information about what their gift will support. Consider crafting targeted pieces featuring one or two E's made to appeal to specific types of donors. (Perhaps millennial donors will be particularly drawn to the library's Engagement area via its cultural programming?) You might also test which E's in particular, and possibly even which categories within those E's, resonate in your donor community.

REACHING THE BUSINESS COMMUNITY

When reaching out to local businesses for support of the library, reference the E's to show how the library is a partner in fostering job skills, creating a strong workforce, supporting entrepreneurs, helping business leaders find resources, and so on.

The E's in Action: Annual Appeals

Annual appeals can be a great opportunity to incorporate The E's of Libraries. (For tips on annual giving campaigns, view the United for Libraries webinar "Annual Giving Campaigns: Best Practices from Across the Country," or read Library Strategies' "14 Important Tips for a Successful Annual Appeal" at http://library strategiesconsulting.org/2016/06/14-important-tips-for-a-successful-annual -appeal). The following is a sample letter from a library Foundation that uses The E's for Libraries to structure its annual funding appeal.

Dear [personal name]:

The Vine County Library Foundation is grateful to include you among the library's supporters. We hope that we can count on you again this year for a generous donation to benefit the library. In 2019, the Vine County Library Foundation has supported the Vine County Library in the areas of:

Education: Through its support of the library's summer reading program, the Vine County Library Foundation reached more than 2,500 local children, providing them with engaging literacy programming and free books.

Engagement: The library hosted a series of city council candidate forums, made possible by funding from the Foundation.

Entrepreneurship: A new Entrepreneur Resource Center at the library, partially funded by the Foundation, is a one-stop shop for those looking to start a business in the community.

Enrichment: The Foundation supported the library's programming around the One City, One Book program, including an author visit, discussion groups, and community outreach.

Exploration: The library's new makerspace in the Young Adult Department, partially funded by the Foundation, enables local high school students to pursue their interests and passions.

We hope you will continue to support this innovative programming that is vital to our community. Please consider a gift of $X or more. Our goal is to raise $50,000 during this appeal. Thank you for your support!

Sincerely,
[signature]

Friends of the Library Groups

MEMBERSHIP APPEALS AND FUNDRAISING

In your Friends group's membership materials and e-mail campaigns, showcase The E's of Libraries and how donations to the Friends provide the "extras" for library initiatives. For example, discuss how summer reading is so important in early Education, and how donations to the Friends support extra programming, free books for children, and additional materials during summer reading.

ENGAGING VOLUNTEERS

The Friends group can identify potential volunteers' interests using "What's Your E?" Someone who is particularly passionate about Employment, for example, might have the skills to volunteer to give one-on-one resume help at the library.

ADVOCACY

If the goal is to engage new members, as it often is with Friends groups, or enliven a group that has been doing the same activities for a long time, a campaign using The E's of Libraries or "What's Your E?" can be a great tool to jump-start the group and its members. Friends who have been doing the same thing for a long time may not even know all the things the library does in so many areas. You can link Friends members to an area in which they are passionate and make them advocates in that area, or recruit new and dynamic members and supporters by appealing to their interest in one of the E's.

State and National Advocacy

The E's of Libraries has been used for statewide legislative days and as a tool for library advocates making the case for increased federal funding. It's also a good fit for a conference theme (for a state library association, a statewide Friends group, etc.)

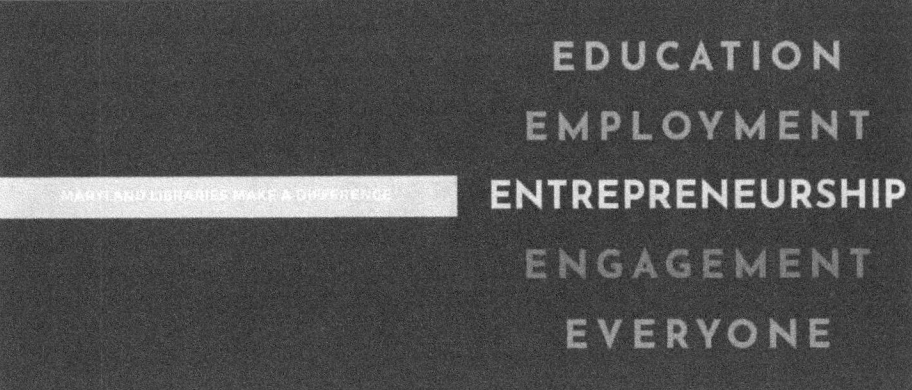

FIGURES 5.2 The Maryland Library Association used The E's of Libraries in its materials for Maryland Library Legislative Day in 2019.

TALKING POINTS *for* ADVOCATES

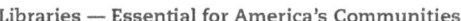

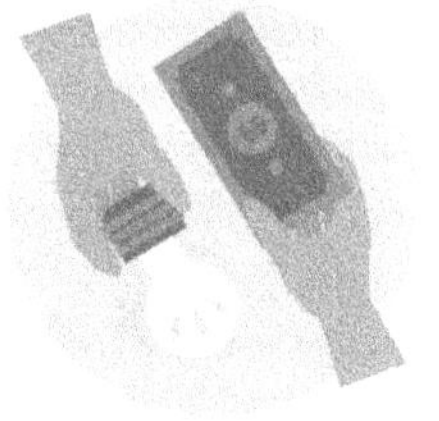

Federal Funding for Libraries

Libraries — Essential for America's Communities

Lawmakers agree: libraries and their services are a national priority. Garnering bipartisan and bicameral support, the **Museum and Library Services Act of 2018** reauthorized the Institute of Museum and Library Services until Fiscal Year 2025.

Despite modest increases for the **Library Services and Technology Act** (LSTA) over the past few years, overall funding remains below levels from the early 2000s. With funding of at least $206 million for LSTA (Congress provided $195.4 million in FY 2020), libraries can launch and sustain urgent and critical services for their communities.

School libraries are supported by **Innovative Approaches to Literacy** (IAL), a competitive grant program administered by the U.S. Department of Education. With at least 50% of grants required to go to school libraries, IAL is the only federal program dedicated to supporting school libraries. IAL grants support literacy materials for young children and training for the most in-need school districts. Access to high-quality literacy programming and resources remains a critical component of childhood literacy.

Congress can continue to enable more than 116,000 public, school, academic, government and other libraries to advance Employment, Entrepreneurship, Education, Empowerment and Engagement (**The E's of Libraries®**) in communities across America.

EMPLOYMENT

- 73% of public libraries assist patrons with job applications and interviewing skills.
- LSTA-funded programs trained school and public librarians to prepare students for today's competitive job market by providing coding classes and other STEM activities.

ENTREPRENEURSHIP

- Nearly 100% of public libraries offer economic/workforce services; about half of those provide entrepreneurship and small business development services.
- LSTA funds allowed entrepreneurs in rural areas to receive business development assistance from a skilled business & technology outreach librarian.

EDUCATION

- 98% of public libraries provide technology training.
- LSTA funds created a virtual reality lab at a university to provide access to emerging technologies for faculty and students.

EMPOWERMENT

- Nearly 100% of public libraries offer no-fee public access to Wi-Fi and computers.
- LSTA funds provided online exam tools at libraries, enabling patrons to improve careers and advance their education.

ENGAGEMENT

- 97% of public libraries help people apply for government services online.
- LSTA funds enabled veterans to claim well-earned benefits to further their education, get medical treatment, start a business and transition to civilian life.

Adapt these points to your location and type of library as appropriate, inserting local examples.

2021 Request

Funding of at least $206 million for LSTA and $27 million for IAL allows more than 116,000 public, school, academic, government, and other libraries to advance employment, entrepreneurship, education, empowerment, and engagement in communities across America.

Please request that your lawmaker:

- Support at least $206 million for LSTA and $27 million for IAL.
- Sign the FY2021 LSTA and IAL appropriations letters when they circulate.
- Visit a library in the district and learn about the services provided to their constituents.

www.ala.org / @ALALibrary ALA American Library Association

For more than 140 years, the American Library Association has been the trusted voice for public, academic, school, government and special libraries, advocating for the profession and the library's role in enhancing learning and ensuring access to information for all. Visit ala.org.

FIGURE 5.3

ALA's Public Policy and Advocacy Office highlighted The E's of Libraries in a piece they crafted that provided talking points to use when advocating for federal funding.

Meeting Your Goals

In your role with the library, what are your key goals?

_____
_____
_____
_____
_____
_____

In what ways can The E's of Libraries or "What's Your E?" help you meet these goals?

_____
_____
_____
_____
_____
_____

For each of the following groups that may be present at your library, list a few ways that they might use The E's of Libraries to meet their goals:

LIBRARY ADMINISTRATION

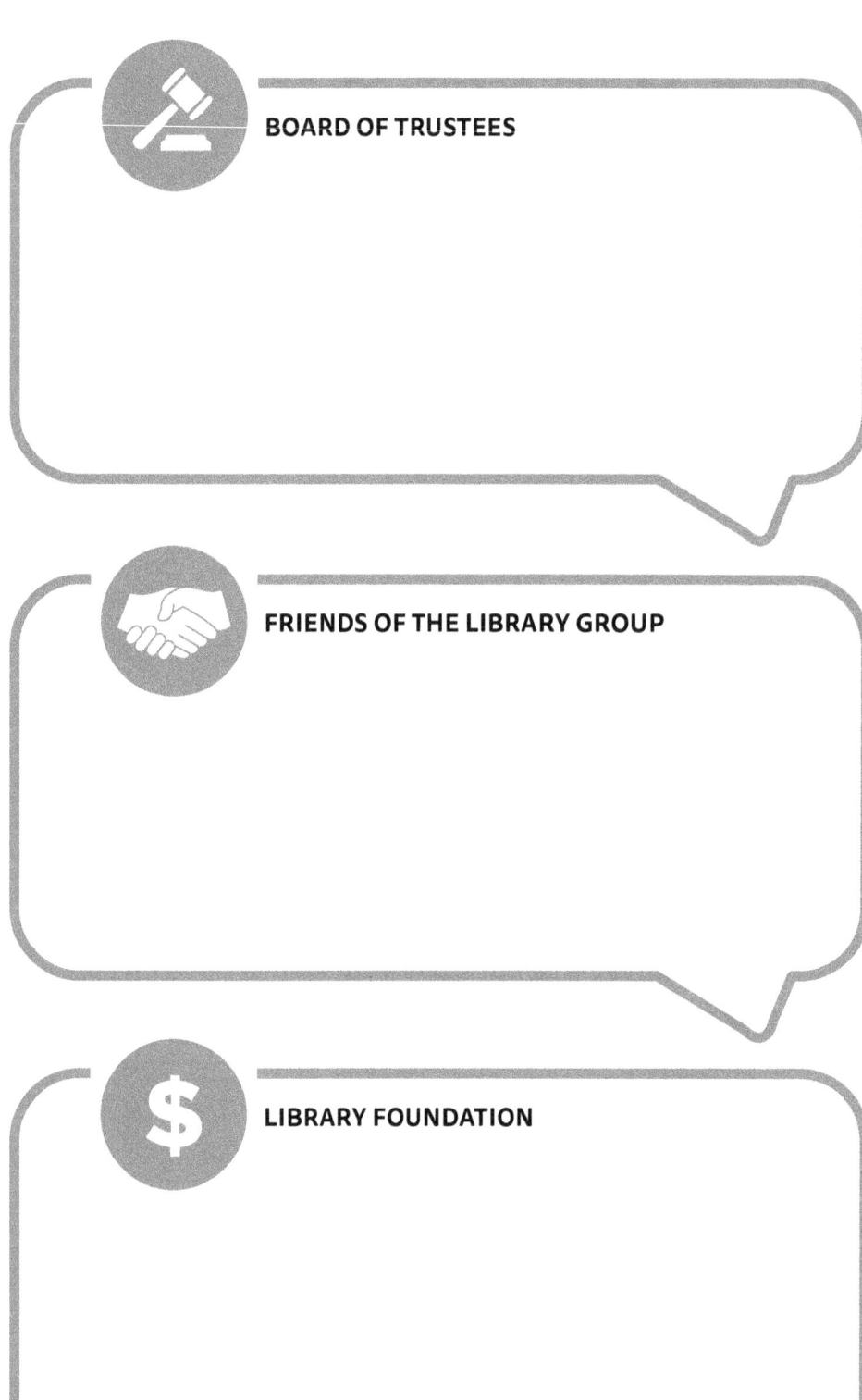

Conclusion
The E's of Your Library and Beyond

WHAT YOU DO AS A LIBRARIAN, LIBRARY ADMINISTRATOR, OR library advocate or supporter is critical on a local, state, and national level. It's our hope that through customizing The E's of Libraries, you will have developed an effective and adaptable framework that will make it easy—and even enjoyable—to prove your library's value to your community and stakeholders.

We hope that you will share all the ways in which you use The E's of Libraries—visit www.ala.org/united/advocacy/es-of-libraries to submit your materials and stories, or e-mail us at united@ala.org. Let us know how we can further support you and your library as you use The E's of Libraries.

Additional Resources

Advocacy Library: www.ala.org/advocacy/advocacy-library

ALA's Public Policy and Advocacy Office: www.ala.org/aboutala/offices/ppa

Civic and Community Engagement: www.ala.org/pla/resources/tools/community-engagement-outreach/civic-community-engagement

The E's of Libraries – I Love Libraries:
www.ilovelibraries.org/education
www.ilovelibraries.org/employment
www.ilovelibraries.org/entrepreneurship
www.ilovelibraries.org/engagement
www.ilovelibraries.org/empowerment

The E's of Libraries—United for Libraries: www.ala.org/united/advocacy/es-of-libraries

Library Advocacy: State and Local Resources: www.ala.org/advocacy/state-local-resources

Project Outcome: www.projectoutcome.org

United for Libraries: www.ala.org/united

About the Authors

ALAN FISHEL is a partner at the law firm of Arent Fox and leads the firm's Communications & Technology group. He has represented the American Library Association on many matters, including at the Federal Communications Commission regarding the proceeding under which the FCC increased the size of the E-rate fund by more than $1 billion annually. Alan also serves on the United for Libraries board, and he is the chair of The E's of Libraries Task Force. In addition, he frequently provides training on a variety of topics, including how to improve advocacy and negotiation skills.

JILLIAN WENTWORTH is the manager of marketing and membership for United for Libraries, a division of the American Library Association. She earned a master's degree in library and information science from Drexel University and a bachelor's degree in English from Hollins University. Jillian has previously worked as a librarian, editor, and journalist. She has presented on library advocacy, working with Friends groups and library trustees, and other topics at national, regional, state, and local library conferences and workshops.

Interested in multiple copies for meetings or trainings?

Go to **alastore.ala.org/action-planner** to learn more about purchasing a cost-effective, downloadable, and print-ready PDF.

ALSO OF INTEREST

All Ages Welcome: Recruiting and Retaining Younger Generations for Library Boards, Friends Groups, and Foundations

A UNITED FOR LIBRARIES ACTION PLANNER

Lina Bertinelli, Madeline Jarvis, Kathy Kosinski, and Tess Wilson

PRINT: 978-0-8389-4742-5

Despite being core library users, millennials and other younger generations are often underrepresented on library boards and library advocacy groups, including Friends groups and Foundations. But you can change that with the help of this planner's hands-on worksheets, brainstorming activities, checklists, and expert advice. Using this toolkit from United for Libraries, you will

- understand generational differences and commonalities through statistics and analysis of Baby Boomers, Generation X, Millennials, and Generation Z/post-Millennials;
- master the ABCs of recruitment and retention, tailoring them to fit your library;
- •craft several customized pitches, giving you confidence no matter the situation or audience;
- work towards defining and managing diversity for your advocacy group; and
- use tried and true methods for successful onboarding of volunteers.

alastore.ala.org/action-planner